I don't need dirty books
  and movies made of sex
    and obscene words
      whispered to me

You don't need
  soft music
    romantic words
      and mushy poetry

So I compromise
  I write erotic poetry
    coming from
      the thoughts

That lie
  snuggled in my mind

I won't use the four-letter words
  and I won't describe the act of sex
    but I'll give you enough
      to make you think

And leave the imagination
  between the lines
    and the mystery
      between my thighs

A Young Woman's Secret Book of Erotic Love Poems

Barbara Farabee

Illustrated by Claudia Ricketts

Celestial Arts
Millbrae, Ca 94030

Copyright © 1974 by Celestial Arts
231 Adrian Road, Millbrae, California 94030

No part of this book may be reproduced by
any mechanical, photographic, or electronic
process, or in the form of a phonographic
recording, nor may it be stored in a retrieval
system, transmitted, or otherwise copied for
public or private use without the written
permission of the publisher.

First Printing, May, 1974
ISBN No.: 0-912310-72-3
Library of Congress No.: 74-9755
Made in the United States of America

3 4 5 6 7 8 9 10 — 80 79 78 77 76

EROTIC LOVE POEMS

If I am to experience
   this thing you call sex
First I must experience
   this thing I call love

*Childish games
    they said we played
        hayrides
            and snowball fights*

*Running through the meadows
    falling down
        laughing
            rolling and tumbling*

They never knew
   the games we played
      after reaching the ground
         were anything but childish

From the first kiss
   till the last gasp
      we were very adult
         leaving childish games behind
            till yet another day

This one night
  of our staying together
    and snuggling
Is worth all those 7,342 nights
    I spent alone
      in my bed

Is there nothing I can say
    or do with you
        in absolute private

We close the bedroom door
    and the walls listen
        as intimate thoughts
            are conveyed

The mirror throws back
    the reflection of us
        lying on the bed

In daylight the birds
    look in
        and at night
            the man in the moon

I feel like we are the cast
    of an underground illicit movie
        with everything around us
            being an audience

Quickly
    draw the blind
        pull the drapes
            lock the door

TURN OUT THE LIGHTS

I am bashful
    you know
        because
            this is
                my very
First time

One man
   one woman
      a kiss
         an embrace

Soft spoken words
   understanding
      gentleness
         wants and needs

Awareness of each other
   touching
      exciting places
        arousing

Passion
  fulfillment
    calm
      and peace

Loving you
  as I know
    you love me

My body hovers over you
  I look into your eyes
    and bend down to kiss you

Oh, such is
  this love
    I feel

I take my fingers
  and stroke your hair
    it is as beautiful
      as the feeling of the wind

Your hand upon me
   is as
      the sun warming my body
         as I melt

Down onto your body
   kissing your neck
      as my hair
         hides my face like a cloud

And protects me
   from the burning reality of man
      and the coldness of phony friends

In you I find all
   I need no more

Keep me safe from harm
   continue loving me

Loving you was like all the things
    Masters and Johnson talked about
        but were never sure existed

Loving you was like falling off
    the edge of the world
        without ever reaching
            the flat corner of earth

It was like the fourth of July
    each time we touched
        and I found the pot of gold
            at the end of the rainbow
                when in your arms

And when we loved

It was a little bit of heaven
    and a little bit of hell
        and the most wonderful thing

That ever happened to my life

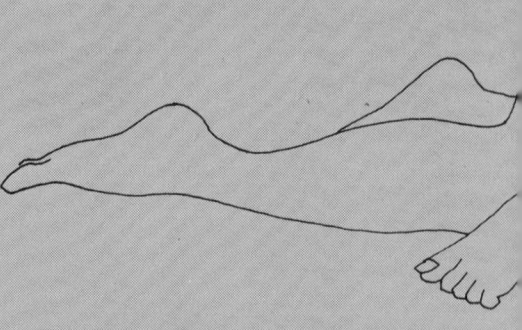

Naked by the sea
  we run hand in hand
    letting the waves
      lick at our feet

The breeze gently
  stroking our bodies
    till the muscles in our legs
      can no longer carry our weight

Falling down beneath
  the yellow moon
    illuminating our bed
      for now

The sand grits between us
  as you move to pull me close
    laughing and lovingly

Our kiss for the time
    as shallow as our breath
        comes quickly and then is gone
            and I lie back to look at you

Is the glow of your face
    reflected only by the moon
        or is it radiant
            from the love we feel

Fall down with me now
    my breathing is even
        until the passion you stir inside me
            causes my breathing to come again
                in shallow gasps

I come to you
  unashamed
    of my nakedness
      before your eyes

I reach out my arms
  to you
    to encircle the love
      of man and woman

And as you pull me close
  I forget we are
    almost strangers
      meeting moments ago

I take your kiss
  and savor your words
    and for the time
      pretend you love me

*I have needed you
    such a long time
        and I cannot risk tomorrow
            and your not being here*

*So come into me
    love me what you can
        and if you find it's not enough
            I'll understand*

But now, the feeling of warm flesh
   against the other
      and kisses that soar my soul
         the feeling of being wanted

These are all I need
   for the moment
      for if you leave
         before even the love of us
            is washed away

These moments will last me
   for many days past
      what you forget
         when you close my door

And I silently lock you
   and the rest of the world away

Remember the night
*   you were so serious*
*   and wanted to be tender*

And everything you did
*   made me laugh*
*   and the sensitive spots you touched*
*   only tickled*

And you kissed me
*   to silence my laughter*
*   and it made me*
*   hysterical inside*

Until
*   you finally shoved*
*   something in my mouth*
*   and I gasped with confusion*

Before
*   I realized it was only*
*   a lollipop*

Then we both laughed

Standing tall above me
  with your face lowering to mine
    blond hair, sunstreaked from the summer sun
      gradually falls on your forehead

Eyes nearly closed
  as eyes meet eyes
    through veiled lashes

And as lips meet lips
  secrets are conveyed
    one to another

Hands now reaching to explore
  secrets that even kisses
    cannot tell

Closeness, so very close
  strong and heavy
    leaning against my body
      pressing manhood against me

My knees are weak
　my emotions high
　　at arms' reach soft flesh
　　　is pulsing beneath my fingers
Pulling you even closer
　to enjoy all the nectar
　　your kisses bring

Your body is warm
    your breath is hot on my face
        your kisses making me
            hunger for more

It lasts only for a moment
    and is over all to soon
        knowing someone may enter the room
            we have shared privately
                only a few kisses ago

Reluctantly arms push back
    though parting is final for the moment
        and we step out from behind the closed door

I remember the touch and kisses
    long after our lips part
        on into the night
            after the secrecy of the day

I sat listening
  patiently
    to an old man

As he watched
  his youth
    go marching by

In young girls
  and loving couples
    aware of no one

But themselves
  and what is contained
    within their world

He told me of
  his misspent youth
    the girls he tossed aside

Never loving
  only using
    too busy

In his bachelorhood
  to stop or pause
    long enough

To know
  what love
    can be

And now he knows
  too late

Tonight, alone in our bed
　I shall reach for you
　　and love you body and soul

Before I grow old
　and find that not only
　　love

But
　sex
　　passed me by

Can't you wait a moment more
   before you have to leave
     I'm unwilling to face
        this night of darkness alone
And stretch my body
   on this big empty bed
     with only the blankets
       to wrap around me
I have become more lonely
   since meeting you
     and my life is without meaning
       when you leave for the night
Can't you wait a moment more
   before you say good-bye
     let me embrace you
       and taste the sweetness of your lips

And when we part
　for a time
　　I'll remember only
　　our kiss
　And I'll not think of your
　soft, soft lips
　　between my thighs

Love in a hammock
is not as easy as it sounds
being careful strangers
don't encounter the scene

Keep your voice down
    so the neighbors won't hear me
        sucking your tongue
            biting your ear

                Keep the hammock from swinging
                  too much from side to side
                      action is gentler
                        it's our thoughts that glide

Oh ecstasy, we're reaching the end
Too late
    you rolled off
        your knee is skinned
Do we have
    to start all over
        on this thing
Again

*She came to me this bright, sun-filled morning
radiant and happy to tell me of her fling
the man she had longed and lusted for
starting many months ago*

*I sat quietly listening to her rush of words
the praise in her voice
and the fire in her eyes
feeling uncomfortable at her display of passion*

*It was John, she said
golden hair and deep blue eyes
a kiss that could shake your soul
and make you hunger for more*

*Her vivid description of his ardent lovemaking
began to shake my world
and the more she talked
the more my world crumbled*

*It was him, my John
whom she knew nothing about
knew nothing of my love for him
and his seeming love for me, I had thought*

*We had argued last night
and he left my side in a rage of fury
saying we would talk again tomorrow night
he later had met her and loved her
never knowing she was my friend*

After, she left, I sat stunned
forgetting everything except my hate
growing and passing the boundaries of my love

My day passed slow and hellish
it took all my courage to ready myself
for our meeting tonight, probably our last
and prepared my words that I would lash out at him

*The doorbell rang as I took my last deep breath
to steady my voice and wipe away the tears from my eyes
The sadness I saw in his eyes
and the shallowness of his voice, as he said, "I'm sorry"*

*Softened my hate, to disillusionment
and without my asking he told me of his downfall
I knew I would never tell him
that she was my friend*

*I couldn't bear to live my life without him
the emptiness I had felt would be small and insignificant
to the life I would face alone without him
when you love, what else could I say, but*

"I forgive you"

Reach out and touch me
   I've been lonely
      for your hand
         enclosing mine

I've been so cold inside
   warm me, please
      your hand feels so warm
         I feel calm inside

Just being this close to someone
      who makes me so happy to be a woman

Thank you, I needed your fingers
   intertwining mine
      now for awhile
         I'll be a little more satisfied

Till once again
   I need you
      to reach out and touch me

You talked so convincingly
  I agreed to go see
    "Deep Throat"

Not to be outdone
  I had to swallow my giggles
    till we got to the show

And I whispered
  all I got on is
    my maxicoat and shoes

Funny
  I can't remember
    what held your attention most

Linda Lovelace
  or me

*Press me closer
    let me feel your strength
        I love the touch
            of your muscled arms*

*And the hardness of your body
    you have spent so much time
        looking after*

*I know each thing you do
    is done vigorously
        but for this time*

*Our time
   and my body
      for all your hardness
         love me tenderly*

I felt you gently stir beside me
    the longing of wanting you
        itching my insides
            tantalizing me

It seems you want me less now
    than in the first few months we met
        but my appetite grows more violent
            to a knot that lies beneath my gut

I want to smother you with wet kisses
    and tease you, with my tender young breasts
        to touch your body
            exploring all your manly charms

Then have you pull me to you
    feeling your passion stirred
        and holding back no longer
            shoving yourself deep inside

Satisfying all my longings
  and ending my frustrations
    but your heavy breathing
      tells me you would rather sleep

Perhaps
  tomorrow night

*Some other time perhaps
I'll fall down
with a man
Who knows my most
erotic place
is my heart
Telling me things
I know are real
feeling the things
I feel
The tender place
on my neck
means little
or nothing
If the touch
is initated only
by sex*

But I still feel
  the tightness
    between my legs
As penetration
  sets it's course
    and you set your goal
Of heavy breathing
  and mere humping
    and nothing more
Till you reach your destination
  of ejaculation
    and murmur only
Let me go to sleep
  leaving me wide awake
The most erotic place
  still untouched

You greeted me with enthusiasm
  as you had so many times before
    your excitement was so exhilarated
      you nearly ripped my coat from me

Sit down on the sofa
  I've something to show you
    I only got it today
      and with that

Took the book and leafed through it hurriedly
  almost tearing the pages
    Let's try this position tonight
      and started to unbutton my blouse

You couldn't understand
  why I abruptly stood up
    and went for my coat

And as I opened the door to leave
  I turned and said
    How many ways can there be
      It's either good or it's bad

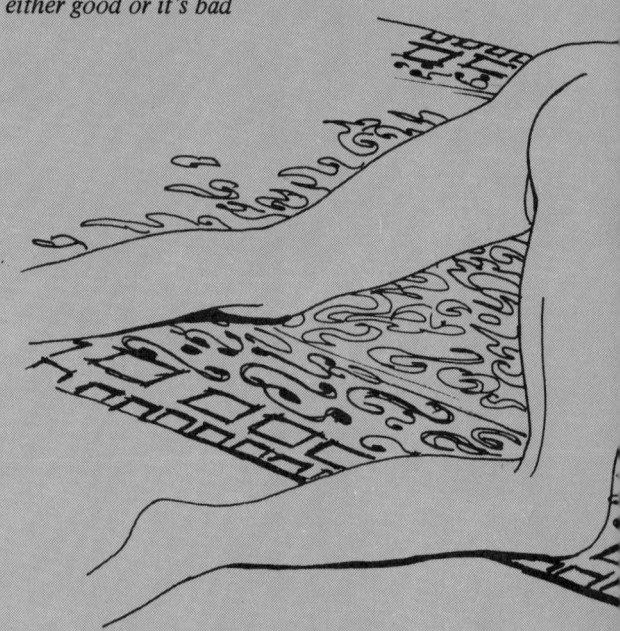

*The silence is deafening
   as I lie on the hard examining table
      with the cold, white, starched sheet
         covering my body*

*I wonder what this new doctor
   will look like and how his hands will be
      as once again the sheet is pulled back
         to expose one breast at a time*

*The minutes tick by slowly
   waiting for the time to begin
      while my heart beats harder and faster
         and my excitement grows*

*He opens the door and calls my name
   and I turn my head slowly to look
      how lucky I chose to come to him
         he's young and the most attractive doctor I've seen*

*He takes my excitement as being embarassment
   and starts the examination, reassuring me
      my eyes close quickly as his hand touches my flesh
         the pounding of my heart reaching his fingertips*

*Pressing lightly, then hard
   around in circles, near my nipple
      covering me completely with his hand
         his voice rattles on, but my mind is full of thoughts*

*Holding onto each touch and adding more
   soon it will be over
      and I'll have to face the world again
         and he'll tell me there's nothing wrong
            something, I already knew*

*It isn't easy being ugly, having no one to care
no one to touch you in intimate places
being gentle and speaking softly*

*This is the fifth doctor I've seen this month
I've been so lonely
and in need of being touched*

*I wonder what will happen first
if I don't find someone to love me
run out of new doctors
or run out of money*

The reflection in the mirror
  shows the change in my face
    my complexion is clear now
      and a smile replaces my frown

My body is void of ugly fat
  and my waistline is trimmer
    than ever before

How proud I'll feel tonight
  in my negligee
    when I greet you at my door

And you see my slim, graceful body
  knowing your love
    has made the change

Moonlight silhouetted her body
   as she raised the window
      gentle breezes caught at her gown
      and draped it to her

The aroma of freshly scrubbed skin
   filled the room
      as she walked to the bed
      to sit beside him

Asleep, she gazed at him
   the moonlight catching the silver
   in his hair
      being unable to remember
         the reason for the argument

Feeling the tenderness rise
   she bent to kiss him
      and as her lips touched
      the coolness of his face

He awoke and pulled her
   to him
   and
      the heat of the argument
      was forgotten

In the heat of his passion

You took me to bed
taking what you wanted
not taking what
I offered to give

Lying with you
    in a bed of sweat
        and each drenched by the other

Mouth to mouth
    belly to belly
        loin to loin
           we love

The pleasures that I feel
    God, but it feels good
        loving you this way

Holding you
    kissing you
        taking passions
            in return for the other

Filling me with your body
    deep inside
        slowly stroking
            until passions can no longer
                hold back the ultimate

Christ,
    it was so good before
        why hasn't it happened again

Summer day at the beach
   the sun tanning my body
      bleaching my hair
         and the sun is so hot
That I dare not move
   from the safety
      of the beach towel
         I lay on
I roll over on my back
   and let the sun bake me
      opening my legs
         exposing my thighs
So they will not resemble
   the creamy, white strips
      of skin
         touched by my bikini
Tonight, I wonder
   will you marvel
      at the contrast
         the light and dark
And the heat of my skin
   the sun has left
      beneath
         the coolness of the sheets
The vulnerability of me
   as sunbleached hair
      frames my face
Or will you be
   as hard and cold
      as before
Slam, bam
   Thank you, ma'am

*Your arm brushed against me
 as you walked past
  and I caught your thoughts
   without looking to you
I know that later
 in the privacy of my home
  the phone will ring
   and you will ask to see me again*

I have told you no before
    that you would only hurt me
        but the way you make me feel
            you know I will say yes again
Maybe this time will be different
    you will love me with your heart
        not just with your body
            and the passions that lie within
My heart quickens
    as I remember the last time
        your body invaded mine
        and I tremble inside
            waiting for your call
I heard your knock on my door
    and tried to hide
        the eagerness on my face
        and without a word
You caught me to you
    and kissed me
        and your arms picked me up
            and carried me to the bedroom
I hid the anger in my voice
    and brushed away the tears
        in my eyes
I wanted you to love me
    not to use me
But as you zipped up your pants
    and buttoned your shirt
        laughed and said
            "Don't call me, I'll call you"
Fooled again

*The lights were dimmed
from glaring white to red
as I entered the door*

*Your voice of hello
was as soft
as the color of the room*

*You took my coat
draping it across the chair
as you embraced me*

*My lips sought yours
eager to push the time and distance away
that had seperated us for so long*

*We knew this was to be the last
of the love affair we had shared
and good-bye would be harder than hello*

*There were words of love, not to be
before our bodies said the parting
in the bedroom of your home*

*You were more gentle than ever before
as your hands re-explored my body they already knew
and your body crushing into mine, would be the last I'd know*

*It was beautiful, this last time I knew you
and so many months have passed
that I cannot recall your face*

*But your name was Chad
and all I can remember now
is the soft, fleshy feel of your buttocks*

*As I held you
and we made love*

Have you forgotten our love
  that we shared
    in the little world
      we created

So far away in time
  before we went
    our separate ways
      building different worlds of our own

Do you ever recall
  girlish giggles
    over something you said
      or did

Reflections in the mirror
  with dark shadows
    of a girl with long, silky hair
      brushing her hair with gentle strokes

*Have you read a poem recently
that resembled one
I wrote to you
telling you of my love*

*The vision of my naked body
slowly sliding into bed
next to you
promising love
has it been forgotten?*

The long talks of future days
    smiling eyes and moistened lips
        a kiss
            renewing our faith in each other

Then came the tears
    and sadness
        and pleading looks
           and muffled cries
              ending it

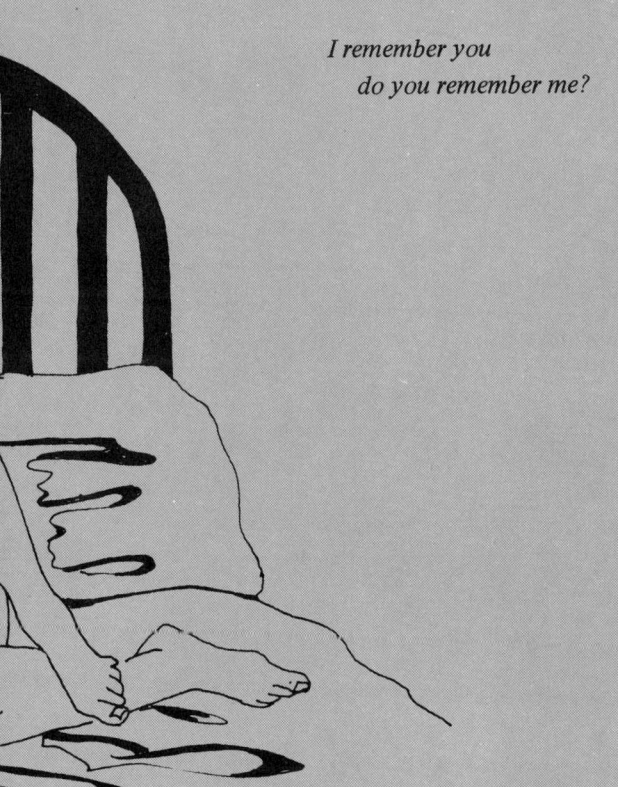

    I remember you
        do you remember me?

Today
    after all tears have been shed
    and the pain has dulled
I will survive
  with you
    or without you
For I love life
  and I won't let
    even you
      take that from me
I'll still laugh
  and smile
    and care about others
I'll cry
  feel sorrow
    and pain
But I will live

*I'll feel sad
 for love is empty
 and over*

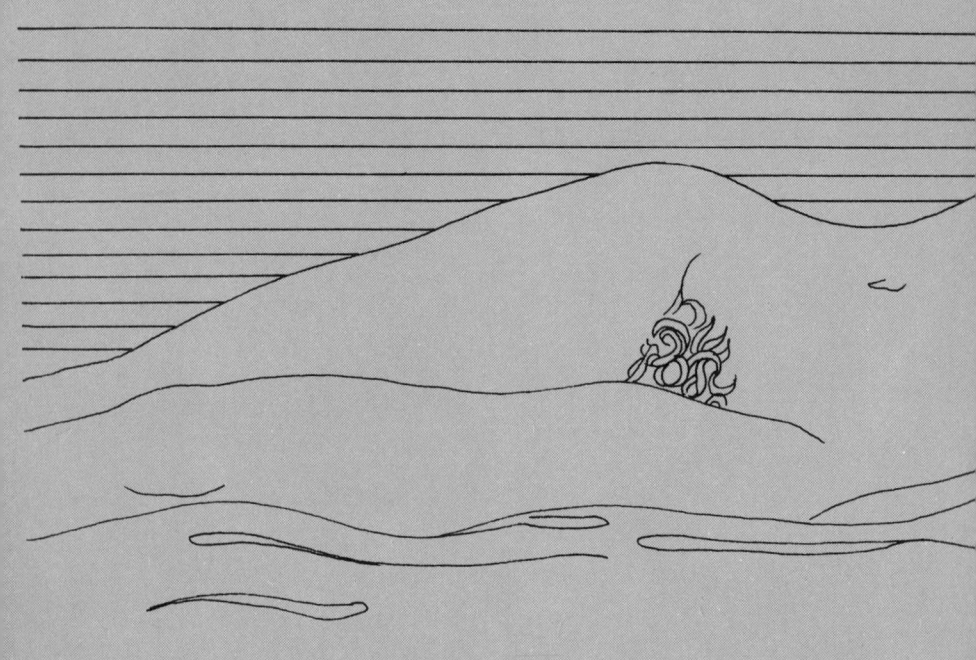

You won't come back to me
I know that now
even if you don't
I only hope
someday in the future
someone else loves you
as I do
And you can return
that love to her
in the same way

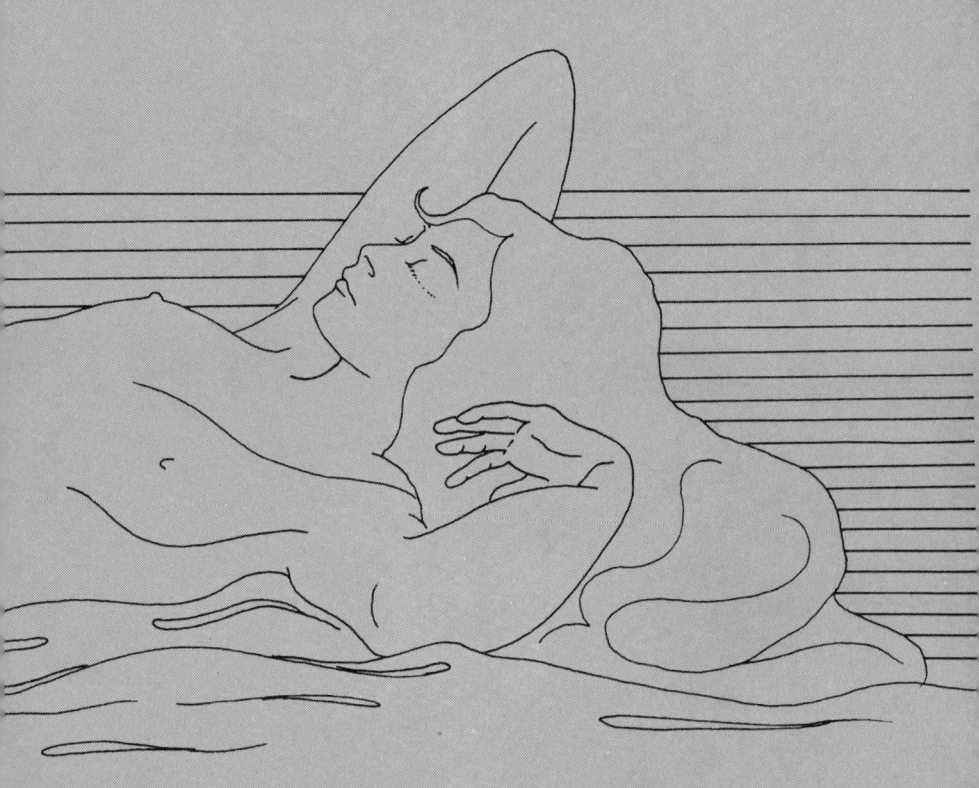

And maybe
  if I'm lucky
    I'll find again
      what I had
        such a long time ago
I won't forget
  the times we spent
    together
I'll look back
  on them now
    and be glad
      for what we had

*And maybe
 just maybe
  someday in the future
   our paths will cross again
And we can recapture
 the love
  that slipped past us
   through this
    sometimes
     miserable and lonely
      life
Till then or ever
 I love you
  however wrong it is
   I will love*

Good-bye
  may you also
    find the beauty and peace
      and the love of life
        and its meaning
          as I have done

It's good to be alive
   for even sadness and hurt
      are part of living
And if the good
   is good enough
      it carries us through the bad times
For I'm left happy
   unafraid of future days

*Because I'm lucky enough
   to know
      even if love happens
      only once
It adds to your life
   even parting cannot
      take away
So don't pity me
   wanting something I cannot have
      I have taken your love
         in return, for that I gave
It leaves me secure
   because I have known
And the only sadness in parting
   I see
      is our love didn't last
      quite long enough
         for you to learn
            to love me*

I am hung up
  strung out
Frustrated
  unhappy
Needing
  wanting
    and not having
Ignored
  and unloved
You can't get
  much satisfaction
Watching other lovers
  love by

*We sat cross-legged
 and nude
  in front of each other*

*Closing our eyes
 and reaching out
  to touch*

It's a game
    and it's not a game
        this exploring

Afterward, they tell us
    we are to know
        each other better

My hand feels
    of your face
        and the stubble of your whiskers

The softness of your skin
    the passion your lips hold
        the gentleness of your eyes

The warmth of your hand
    travels up my arm
        to rest on my shoulder
            as your fingers fondle my hair

You become aware
    of my deep and heavy breathing
        as the chemistry between us
            stirs our passions

Your hand slowly moves
    to my chest
        to feel the rise and fall
            of the intake and outlets of air

You bend toward me
    placing your lips
        on my bare breasts
            to feel the sensation fully
                of the softening to hardening
                    of my nipples

I am excited as never before
    a passion possesses me with no control
        the game of sensory touch is over

I am ready to make love

Tongues probing
    teeth biting
        arms reaching
            hands groping
Tender flesh
    hard flesh
        roughness
            and smooth
Gulps of air
    a sigh
        a tremor
            passion consuming

Covers kicked aside
   bed springs squeaking
     thrusting
       lying still
Hot and sweaty
   frustration stilled
     weakness claiming
       our bodies
Words of love
   a good-night kiss
     snuggling
       before sleep sets in

I have seen you often
  half naked by the sea
    running and joking
      swimming as
        your arms cut through

The water
  skimming half above
    and half below
      and floating gracefully
        as if lying on solid ground

You have walked past me
   so slow and so close
      I could almost count each hair
         that adorns your chest

And those that stream down
   past your chest
      past your hard belly
         to the brief trunks that hide you

I have fought the urge to look
   too intently
      at the bulge you proudly display
         and flaunt before me
            teasingly

I have imagined the soft down of hair
   that protects your most
      precious treasures of all
         being at my fingertips

And now
>after all the many years
>>I've wondered
>>>how you would look nude

I open a book
>and there you are
>>so naked, so sexy
>>>so manly

*It may not matter to you
 that a certain red-haired girl
  enjoys the thought
   of possessing your body*

*But it matters to me
I'm glad you were in
 The Centerfold*

I turn to him silently in the night
    when the pangs of loneliness become
        too great a burden to bear

I kiss him softly
    while the lips I am kissing
        are a fantasy of yours

The arms of him who encircle my body
    are remembered in other places
        where yours have been

I say words of love
    while it is you who I talk to
        but you never know

And when it ends
    I cry silently in desperation
        it was not you I loved
            only the memory of you
                in someone else's body

How heavy are the chains of love
    when someone else must carry them
        other than the one you love

Ha, you think you're such a man
   so confident with your smirk
      that you've forgotten what a smile is
You are the one who knows how
   to please a woman
      an orgasm more
And your very presence is enough
   to make her want you
      and if she is lucky
         you may grant her the favor
Of your fabulous body
   and the privilege
      of bedding down with you

After all, it's not just any girl
   you choose
      your being so damn particular
You'll tell her
   she's the greatest
      you've ever had
         and come back again
When you have the time
   to work her into the busy schedule
      of all your other lady friends
Naive and stupid
   I thought you were who
      I was looking for

Your good looks
    your sauveness and charm
        and all of your jet-set friends
I knew the others had to be wrong
    the things they said
        so I fell for you
Believed you
    wanted you
        was excited by you
But your phony act
    before and after
        showed me the real man
Believe me
    for all your self-love
You're the worst lay
    I ever had

I look past your lips
   which have just spoken to me
      and look at your body
         your manhood which still
            lies weak and unrisen

My fingers tremble
   as I reach to your chest
      and fumble with the buttons
         that close away
            the dark mat of hair beneath

I lean toward you heavily
   as excitement makes me weak
      you smell of a hard days' work
         and the stubble of your breard
            scratches against my face

Lips finally meet
   and I thrust my tongue
      deep inside your mouth
         trying to raise the passion in you
         as you have done to me

Our heavy breathing seemed
   to have taken eternities to begin
   and now you have finally
      forgotten your "no"
         and let your desire rise
         to meet mine

My hand moves to your lap
   and I feel the hardness of you
      hiding under layers of soft cloth
      I look to your eyes and know
         your body overpowers your mind

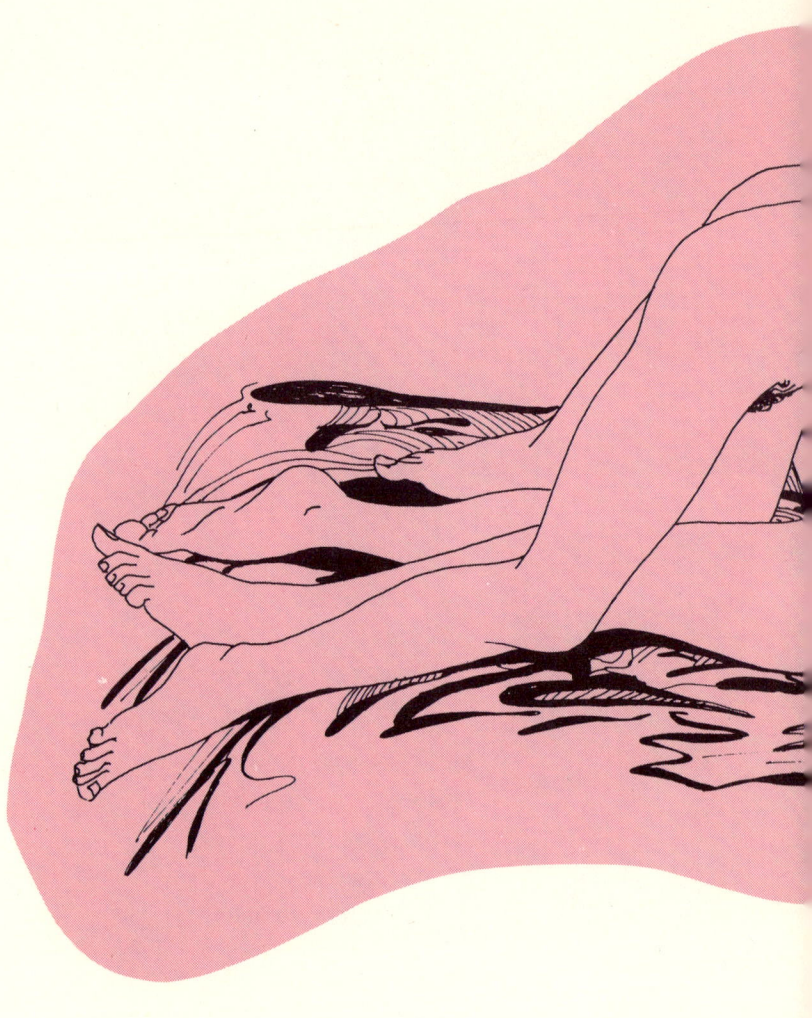

I take your body
   and the pleasures that it gives
      caring not that when lovemaking ends
         you will leave without words of love
      and tell the ones you know
         how I seduced you again

I am shameless
    A woman with no scruples
        I care not about the words of later
            only of now

And your body crushing mine
    into the bed
        and the mattress wrapping around me
            I wanted you and had you

I win again

•

What do you know of love
    besides the dirty words
        you scribble
            on bathroom walls

And the pictures of nudity
    and men and women together
        in positions
           that don't even resemble sex

*All the underground movies
and stag parties you go to
the paperback books
you hide in your drawers*

*The high-browed looks
to the young girls
who pass by*

*What do you know of love
when you don't even know of sex*

The bed springs squeak
    behind the paper thin wall
        next to where I lay

I know now that
    there is someone else with you
        rocking with your body
            giving pleasures I once did

Muffled laughter
    and tiny moans of love
        pound against my eardrums
            driving me crazy with jealousy

I know I should go to the other room
    turn on the tv and shut the noise away
        but I don't want you to know
            that I hear your love-making with her

Oh, how I hate you, for the pain you bring
    my lover in the next apartment
        when I used to be the
            Lay, Lady, Laid
                across your big brass bed

Where are you ecstasy
   I have searched between the legs
      of many men

In the expensive
   and the cheap rooms
      of hotels and motels

There has been
   nothing left untried
      no words
         left unspoken

And still
   after I've laid
      with the next new man

The aroma of sex
   in my nostrils
      makes the frustrations
         increase more

Where is ecstasy?

Did you take lessons
   in being so crude
      does every word that
         comes from your mouth

Have to be the filth
   and the slime
      I knew in the
         poor and trashy

Neighborhood
   I grew up in
      before the

Chance to leave
   and be a person
      me
         a woman with dignity

*I'm tired of four-letter
 words
  about sex*

*Why can't someone
 just be man enough
  to use the
   four-letter word*

LOVE

Smile
  awhile
Play
  stay
Love me
  leave me
Same old shit

I have gone through men
as if they would be there
throughout my lifetime
My world is growing older
and it is time to love one
than to use many

*Gone, many miles from where I can
reach out to you and pull you
close to me
Not much fills my time now
working to get me through the days
thoughts of you to get me through the nights
I fill my evenings with music
that we have listened to together
and I take the music and wrap it around me
shutting away some of the cold and loneliness
that only you can take away completely*

*And when I go to bed and become restless
I close my eyes and see your smiling face
and I go to sleep eager
for the morning to come
taking me closer to the time
when we are together again
Hurry back, my love
for I am lonely without you
and my lips are eager for your kisses
and my arms are in need of wrapping around you
and my body longs for the closeness of yours*

Take me in your arms gently
when I come to you
kiss me tenderly as you pull me close
tell me you have missed me
as I have been missing you
fill the room with the softness of music
and let us drink in the joy that surrounds us
let us love together before words are spoken
for I need the warmth your body brings to me
and the happiness that fills my heart
when I am with you

*I am so lonely now
take your hand and brush it away
fill my whole being with yourself
so that I am whole again
and when we fulfill this part of ourselves
let me lie quietly in your arms
for a moment or two
being able to hold onto it long enough
to last until the next time
your bed becomes full
of two people embracing in love
once more
lonely and empty
I wait eagerly
for your return*

My face reddened
   as your eyes took over my body
      I felt embarrassed
         as the layers of clothing
Were peeled away
   and you undressed me
      with only your eyes
It took only the movement
   of your lips and tongue
      to make me quiver and tingle inside
It was hard acting poised
   as if I hadn't noticed
      carefully I wiped the sweat from my palms
         and crossed my legs
Fighting the heavy feeling
   of frustration
      gradually growing inside my groin
My arms cross over my
   small and tiny breasts
      as if to protect them
         from invasion of your mind
Then you turned
   and walked away

It happened many years ago
  but I remember the feeling well
    and even though I have never
      seen you again
During those moments
  I feel unwanted by anyone
    and sexy is always
      someone else
Thank you
  Stranger
    you made me feel
      like a woman
Again today

Wings of my lover
    so soft, that touch me
        as light as a gentle breeze
How heavy can wings
    of a lover be
        when they are only
Fantasy?

OTHER CELESTIAL ARTS/LES FEMMES BOOKS YOU WILL ENJOY:

In NEW POETS:/WOMEN, Terry Wetherby has gathered a powerful collection of poetry by the best of the emerging women writers. Voices from the ghetto, suburbia, the country, the city: all are here, speaking out of a great variety of age and ethnic groups and educational levels. 160 pages, soft cover, $4.95

The affirmations set forth in I DESERVE LOVE give you the power to achieve whatever goals you pursue. Defining an affirmation as a positive thought that you choose to immerse in your consciousness to produce a desired result, Sondra Ray presents specific exercises in a variety of areas, including sex, love, self-esteem, affection, and trust, to name a few. 128 128 pages, soft cover, $3.95.

Far from being limited to women, the Equal Rights Amendment (ERA) will dramatically affect 100% of the population, both directly and indirectly. IMPACT ERA is the first and only book to predict ways in which the ERA will affect individual rights, employment, education and domestic relations, both legally and socially. Edited by the California Commission on the Status of Women. 288 pages, soft cover, $4.95.

HOW CAN I SHOW THAT I LOVE YOU? by Elisa Bowen combines words and photographs to show how mates and lovers can demonstrate the tender feelings they have for one another. Chapters on massage, bathing, exercising, playing, talking, cooking, and celebrating show how to renew the glow of courtship by tuning up the senses to see, hear, feel, the one we love. 8½x11, 128 pages, soft cover, $4.95.

Although her personal life has been stalked by tragedy, Joy Simmons has come through with determination and hope and has written a collection of poetry that is powerful, tender, tough, and above all, totally honest. THIS OF JOY reflects the unrelenting reality of life: there is no air of innocence, but there is an essence of beauty, of sweetness, and of optimism that permeates every line. 96 pages, soft cover, $3.95.

If nothing else is ever written about the pain and joy of being female, Elizabeth Avakian's TO DELIVER ME OF MY DREAMS will serve to tell the story. "It takes time and energy to stay in touch with all my parts and with someone else as well, but for me, at least, the two seem to nourish each other, as long as I feel free to be all the different people I discover I am." 96 pages, soft cover, $3.95.

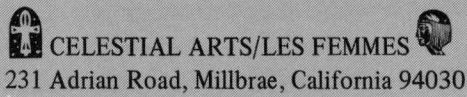

CELESTIAL ARTS/LES FEMMES
231 Adrian Road, Millbrae, California 94030